HAUNTED OBJECTS

Grace Ramsey

Rourke
Educational Media

rourkeeducationalmedia.com

Guided Reading Level: N

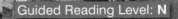

Scan for Relat
and Teacher

JAN 17

TABLE OF CONTENTS

Strange Objects

Normally, dolls need people to move them. Chairs do nothing but sit still. And paintings simply hang on walls without any effect on their environments.

A rocking chair begins moving. No one is sitting in it. Is it the wind? Or something supernatural?

But when these and other objects behave strangely, some people think, "Yikes! It's haunted!"

Throughout history, there have been many claims of haunted objects. Some think spirits can attach themselves to objects that were significant to them in life.

Some think it's possible for unhuman **entities**, such as demons, to attach themselves to ordinary objects.

People who claim to experience hauntings sometimes say their TVs and other electronics turn on and off on their own.

PARANORMAL PLAYTHINGS

Dolls are beloved by children all over the world. But sometimes these toys get bad **reputations.**

Some dolls, for example, have been examined after extraordinary events were blamed on their presence. These dolls are thought to be cursed or **possessed** by a spirit.

Mandy, a doll made in the early 1900s, cried every night, according to the woman who owned it. The sound of its wails echoed through the childless house, waking its owner, who finally gave the doll away.

In the late 1800s, a young boy received a handmade doll from a family servant. Soon, strange things began happening. Objects were thrown across the room. Other toys were destroyed. Family members felt threatened. The boy began insisting that his family call him by his middle name, Gene, because the doll was the real Robert. He also insisted Robert was to blame for all the bad things that happened. Robert is now on display at East Martello Museum in Key West, Florida. Robert's legend grew more famous after the *Child's Play* film series was based on it.

Mandy is now kept in a glass case at Quesnel & District Museum in Canada. The staff says the doll bangs on the glass and will destroy any doll that is placed near it.

The crying stopped at the home once Mandy was gone.

SPIRITED FURNITURE

You can probably look around and see at least one chair right now. You may even be sitting in one. What if that chair was haunted?

The chairs at Belcourt Castle in Rhode Island don't welcome visitors with open arms. An icy chill is felt by those who dare to get close to them. People who try to sit

Banquet Hall at Belcourt Castle

on them claim to encounter **resistance** from an unseen force.

Belcourt Castle is also reported to house a haunted mirror, a possessed statue, and a screaming suit of armor.

The Busby Stoop Chair, owned by convicted murderer Thomas Busby, is rumored to be cursed by his **vengeful** spirit. The chair remained in the Busby Inn after he was hanged for his crime in the 1700s.

People who sat in the chair were often involved in **fatal** accidents. In 1978, the chair was moved to the Thirsk Museum in North Yorkshire.

No one has sat in it since.

IF WALLS COULD TALK

Mirror, mirror on the wall, who's behind me in the hall?

When you're brushing your teeth in the morning, you don't expect to see anyone other than your family appear in the mirror around you.

A mirror at the Roosevelt Hotel in Hollywood, California, is rumored to be haunted by the legendary Marylyn Monroe. Guests and staff say they see her reflection looking back at them.

At the Myrtles Plantation in Louisiana, you may catch a glimpse of the spirits rumored to be stuck inside its famous mirror.

The plantation, built in 1796, now operates as a bed & breakfast and hosts daily tours.

The Myrtles Plantation is considered one of America's most haunted houses. Many deaths occurred there. Photographs of the mirror appear to show multiple handprints, which seem to come from the opposite side of the glass. The glass has been cleaned and replaced, but the handprints still appear.

Paranormal enthusiasts come from all over to stay at the plantation, hoping to experience its reported hauntings.

In some cultures, people cover the mirrors in a home when someone passes away. This is done so the deceased's soul will not be trapped inside one.

When you think of art, do you think of ghosts? Most people don't. But there are a few works of art that have scared up spirited rumors.

Some paintings are said to come to life in the night. Others bring spirits into the homes where they hang.

The Internet is teeming with stories of haunted paintings. Some have been blamed for causing illness and death.

The Anguished Man was an unwanted gift. It was considered evil and kept stored away. When the original owner died, her grandson took the painting to his home. He didn't believe there was anything to the stories his grandmother told.

Shortly afterward, the man and his wife began seeing a shadow figure in their home. They also heard crying from a corner of a room. The painting has traveled to many reportedly haunted locations, where paranormal investigators say it has interacted with other spirits.

The Crying Boy is said to set homes ablaze. In several accounts of destroyed homes all over Europe, firefighters sifting through the rubble have found a copy of this late 1960s painting of a young boy with a tear rolling down his cheek.

In each case, the portrait is unharmed, though the house is burned to the ground.

SPOOKY THREADS

Clothes can't be haunted.
Can they?

There's a wedding dress in
Pennsylvania that witnesses
say shakes and sways in its
glass case. The dress was
picked out by young Anna
Baker, before her father forbid
her to marry the man she
loved. Anna never married.

The Baker Mansion is a historic home in
Pennsylvania built between 1844 and 1848.

She died in the family home in 1914. The home became a museum, and the dress was put on display. According to some accounts, the dress shakes so violently, museum staff fear it might break the glass.

Visitors and staff claim they've seen the ghosts of both Anna and her father in the mansion.

WHAT CAUSES A HAUNTING?

Objects believed to be haunted can be new or old. They can be works of art, tools, chests, jewelry, and even toys.

But what turns an ordinary, everyday object into something spooky?

One theory is that a living person had a strong attachment to the object at one time. The energy from that person transferred to the object.

If the energy was negative, or the person was violent, the hauntings take on a more **sinister** nature.

Can objects really be haunted? Or might overactive imaginations be responsible for reports of paranormal activity?

What do you *believe?*

Haunted objects are often sold to collectors. In 2015, a man auctioned a laptop he claimed was possessed after leaving it at a graveyard overnight.

STUDYING THE PARANORMAL

Paranormal researchers aren't just after spooky thrills. The purpose of investigations is to capture evidence that can help further our understanding of supernatural phenomena. These investigations are also done sometimes to give peace of mind to someone who thinks they are being haunted.

Paranormal researchers always get permission before investigating a property.

A good researcher will always look for a natural explanation first when investigating a reported haunting.

Want to learn more about hauntings, and the tools and methods paranormal investigators use?

Check out these websites:

http://kids.ghostvillage.com

www.scaryforkids.com/true-stories

www.paranormalghost.com/ghost_hunter_101.htm

GLOSSARY

entities (IN-tuh-tees): things with distinct and independent existences

fatal (FAY-tuhl): causing or leading to death

paranormal (PAR-uh-nor-muhl): events or phenomena that are beyond the scope of normal scientific understanding

possessed (PUH-zest): controlled by an evil spirit

reputations (rep-yuh-TAY-shuhns): worth or character as judged by others

resistance (ri-ZIS-tuhns): the act of resisting or fighting back; a force that opposes the motion of an object

sinister (SIN-iss-tuhr): giving the impression that something harmful or evil is happening or will happen

vengeful (venj-full): seeking to harm someone in return for a perceived injury

INDEX

SHOW WHAT YOU KNOW

1. What are some reasons people think an object can be haunted?

2. What reasons do believers think might lead a spirit to attach to an object?

3. Is it possible for a new object to be haunted?

4. What kind of object do you think is the creepiest?

5. What do you think about ghosts and hauntings? Are they real or imagined?

About The Author

Grace Ramsey is a journalist, author, and mega-fan of paranormal research shows. She once joined a crew of investigators at one of the world's most haunted places. Her experiences there made her much less skeptical of the supernatural. She still gets the chills just thinking about that night. Yikes!

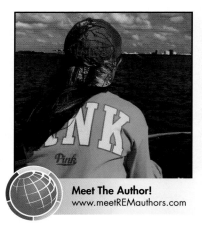

Meet The Author!
www.meetREMauthors.com

Though there has been plenty of research done by believers and skeptics alike, there is no definitive scientific proof that ghosts are real. This series explores the stories of hauntings as told by those who claim to have experienced them. The publisher and authors do not endorse any claims herein as fact.

PHOTO CREDITS: Cover/Title Page © Rob Kirby; Page 4 © Sharon Dominick, Lukiyanova/frenta; Page 5 © Xavier Arnau; Page 6 © Fernando Alvarez Charro; Page 7 © dmitris kolyris; Page 8 © Phil McDonald; Page 9 © ANTONIS LIOKOURAS; Page 11 © Robert Chew; Page 12 © Bonciutoma; Page 13 © Charles V. Hamm, Michael Neelon (tourism)/Alamy Stock Photo; Page 14 © www.hauntedrooms.co.uk; Page 15 © THE INFAMOUS BUSBY STOOP CHAIR IN THIRSK MUSEUM; Page 16 © ZORAN IVANOVIK; Page 17 © TammyMehl; Page 18-19 © Morgan Moss; Page 20 © Yaroslav Gerzhedovich; Page 21 © Steve Kipping; Page 22 © Jozef Goossens/Jeu Wijnen; Page 23 © Erin Wilkins; Page 24 © Pubdog, Emily Dimov-Gottshall; Page 25 © Explore Altoona; Page 26 © shauni; Page 27 © Heidi Freichs; Page 28 © mariusFM77; Page 29 © Dieter Spears

Edited by: Keli Sipperley
Cover and interior design by: Jen Thomas

Library of Congress PCN Data

Haunted Objects / Grace Ramsey
(Yikes! It's Haunted)
ISBN (hard cover)(alk. paper) 978-1-68191-759-7
ISBN (soft cover) 978-1-68191-860-0
ISBN (e-Book) 978-1-68191-949-2
Library of Congress Control Number: 2016932720

Also Available as:

ROURKE'S e-Books